More praise for Theory of Impact

In her new book, *Theory of Impact*, Lisa Sullivan digs deep into questions of trauma and abuse, the pain of not having children, and the speaker's conflicted feelings for a disabled Marine Veteran father. In "The Childless Mother," she tells us of "...my only picture of you, / a black-and-white ultrasound, now faded / to a shade of bruise," brilliantly highlighting the heartbreak it is impossible for the speaker to let go of. But the poet also writes of love and hope. In the beautiful "Against Desire," she reminds us that new growth often comes from decay: "*...with time, out of the muck, / the sulfurous air, / grows grace.*" This is an important collection of verse, for what is art if not our ability to sing of our pain. And while the speaker's pain is often palpable here, every page sings.
—**Brian Mosher**, author of *Relict* and *A Muster of Melodious Musings*

Beyond sun-bleached grief, trauma is triggered in *Theory of Impact* "as quick as a scythe / to the ankles of cornstalks." This debut collection is as intricately shaped as sea-washed shells, revealing scar patterns carved into each loved one. Sullivan sifts the debris of family dysfunction and loss to "learn how to let go of letting go?" In the mother-daughter relationship, the speaker is at times, her mother's "irritant / that starts the pearl." Yet, it's the father's ghost the daughter wrestles with throughout, muscle memory trading "the sting of his steel-toe boot" for a chance to catch praise reflected from his "steel-blue eyes." The rusted memories become "ancient dolmens, / abandoned trackways" that, when mined, remind us, "this is what time smells like: Musk and ivory."
—**Jenifer DeBellis**, author of *Warrior Sister, Cut Yourself Free* and host of Restore Your Inner Warrior

Theory of Impact

Lisa J. Sullivan

LILY POETRY REVIEW BOOKS

Library of Congress Control Number: 2026940889

Cover design and layout: Michael McInnis.
Image from the collection of the author, used with permission.

ISBN: 978-1-957755-77-9

Published by Lily Poetry Review Books
223 Winter Street
Whitman, MA 02382
lilypoetryreview.blog/

For all the late roses.

Contents

so many bleeding hearts 3
Late Rose 4
My father drew maps 5
Mum says don't swallow gum or it will stay in your stomach
for seven years 6
Drive-In 7
Choreography 8
Bread Crumbs 9
Theory of Impact 11
dying maple leaf – 13
350s 14
Northern Lights 15
Winter Thunder 16
To the Bog of Allen 17
Highbush Blueberries 19
On Coquina Beach 20
off balance – 24
Rust 25
Blight 26
Fishing 27
Shift 29
My brother named his sons after our father 31
Sea Glass 32
Home 33
they say we do not 38

Pointillism 39
Nocturne 40
The Childless Mother 41
Dragonflies 43
A Childless Woman Creates Her Family Tree 44
Nesting Season 45
Against Desire 46
anniversary visit – 47
On Any Bay 48
-ectomy 49
Parts of a Letter 50
Acknowledgments 60
Special Thanks 61
About The Author 62

Theory of Impact

so many bleeding hearts
on one slender stem –
a broken home

Late Rose

It is unseasonably warm
at October's end, the garden –
spent, but for periwinkle asters,
a stunted pink rose that teeters
in my line of vision.

Rose – my mother's middle name.
She winces as she sits across
from me. I ask when her
back pain began. She takes
a quiet sip of tea.

What she shares next –
a secret long in her marrow,
kicks away another pebble
of respect that remains
for my father –

his steel-blue eyes
traded for the sting
of his steel-toe boot.

My father drew maps

complete with rivers, roads,
swirls of elevation.

I think to him, a disabled
Marine Veteran, they led
to somewhere beyond the front
door he could no longer open.

These maps were never
painted, never inked –
he always drew them in pencil

and he would erase, erase,   erase.

Mum says don't swallow gum or it will stay in your stomach for seven years

I peel gum from the sidewalk,
pop it in my mouth, ignore the grit.
            There is some sweetness left.

When asked where
I got it, I hide it between
my cheek and baby teeth.

I even keep it in my mouth
when I nap, though Mum
also told me never to do that.

For dinner, again we pick
dandelions in the backyard,
catch crayfish from the brook.

I eat the bitter salad, refuse
the meat, retrieve my gum
from beneath the Formica table.

            The sweetness is gone.
I think of another place to stick the wad –
on a park bench, the apple tree trunk,

the tar-coated telephone pole –
because I can't swallow it.
I just can't.

Seven years is a long time.

Drive-In

He told us to hide
in the wheel wells
of the old Impala, my
brother and me, to save
two dollars apiece
at the drive-in. We did
as we were told, being
the smallest of four
in the cavernous back
seat. But I could tell
by the quiet tightness
in Dad's voice – this was
something we weren't
supposed to do. We
were taught never to lie
in Sunday school. Dad
himself warned us – God
punishes people for lying.
He paid the fee, we rolled
through the open gates,
gravel spitting in our wake.
"You can come out now,"
Dad called, as the glowing
end of his cigarette lit
the green mosquito coil.
We crawled onto the roof,
free and wild to the night sky.
A million of God's eyes
twinkling upon us.

Choreography

From my hiding place
in the cupboard, I spied
my parents' shadows
dancing across the kitchen wall.

Was that a rose held
between my mother's teeth?
A bow tie at my father's neck?

A song in her voice?

A sway?
A twirl?
A lift?
A stumble?

Years later, I understand –
it wasn't the Salsa.
It wasn't the Lindy Hop –
not the Tango's seductive dip.

It was a gasp,
a flail,
the yank
of my mother's hair.

Bread Crumbs

Rooms separate us – he
in the den – I
quiet in the kitchen.
We're not allowed to bother him
while he sleeps – a deep,
medicated sleep that even
his cigarettes can't smoke out.

The couch creaks
beneath his shifting weight.
I jump up to greet him,
but Mum whispers – *Not yet!*
Give him time to wake.

I sit for two long minutes – tiptoe
toward the den – peek in. He palms
the edges of a record album,
lumbers to the turntable, kneels
before it as if to pray.

The acoustic guitar chords
of Bread release
                    my held breath.
A duet begins – Dad's bass vibrato
with the tenor of David Gates.

> *Hey, have you ever tried...*
> *really reaching out for the other side...*

I drift in – freeze when he sees me.
He doesn't stop singing –
                                        but smiles.

I sing, too.

Theory of Impact

Something has changed
my aunt's voice.
It cracks, heaves on the phone.
She asks to speak
to my older brother.

I hold my breath
in the next room, twirl the frayed
ends of my hair,
listen
to his silence.

He hangs up the phone, trudges
into the living room as if through

deep snow.

And somehow I know.

Is he dead?

Yes.

Hit-and-Run Drunk Driver Kills
Disabled Veteran in Crosswalk
Body hurled 75 feet on impact.

Our father: D.O.A. – 2 A.M.

His killer gets six months in jail,
while we kids get
a week off from school. We return,
try to learn the Periodic
Table of Elements, geometry,
composition,

the Theory of Impact.

dying maple leaf –
its new pattern
a butterfly

350s

—for Johnny

My little brother is a budding mechanic.
He buys shitbox cars, parks them
on the foot-high lawn, tinkers under
their hoods all day while I'm in school.
He works on junk motorcycles, too,
then sells them for a profit.

Of course, the neighbors complain
about living next to a "used-car lot" –
about the 8 a.m. roars of muffler-less
exhaust giving tremors to the coffee
in their cups, about the gas fumes
floating on their Charles River breezes.

Grandma once pounded her German fist
and joked –
Oh, he fixes cars...for good!

One day, a rusty radiator explodes –
melts the skin off Johnny's torso.
He lies fetal in a tub of ice water
until Mum arrives and rushes
her six-foot baby to the hospital.

Weeks later, my bandaged brother
buys a rusty '70 Chevelle – tells me,

The body might be junk,
but 350s never die...

Northern Lights

My grandfather claimed
to have seen the Northern Lights
in Nova Scotia in 1949.

I travel there – to Lunenburg, where
our ancestors arrived in 1752 – this land
of a hundred lakes, stillwaters, trout streams,
moose, marten, and black bear –
where sugar maples, birch, and hemlock
preside over foxberry, wood sorrel,
sarsaparilla.

I hike the drumlins and eskers
to higher ground and wait for night.
Grandpa was right. In the sky,
emerald streaks curl into fuchsia,
turquoise, reach as if to embrace me,
my mouth flared open like a bell –

This is the light I remember
in Grandpa's eyes.

Winter Thunder

Great Grandma said it means
there will be snow in seven days –

or there will be frost in May.
She'd ring a hand bell

to ward the thunder away –
burn a candle until it passed.

My mother never asked
what evil that prevented.

I prefer to think of winter thunder
as a displaced thing that asserts itself –

like a bullied child who's had enough,
and marches across a field

of dormant heather, emboldened
by the sound of his sudden, booming voice.

To the Bog of Allen

Written in response to the video short *"Into the Mire"* by Nigel Rolfe, for The Poetry Project – Ireland

You are lonely because
you claim the lonely –
ancient dolmens,
abandoned trackways,
restless folk who fail
to check your depth
before they step.

But I saw that man
who stood on the edge
of your edge
and fell like a domino
into what he thought
was a part of himself.

Your typical lure –
he mistook a water ripple
for a weary mouth
pleading, *Help*.

You have always lain
between two sides
of a thing:
The Liffey – The Shannon.
They feed you
even when you aren't hungry.

Did you let him rise
because you had no appetite?
Or have you learned to tell
the difference between
those who come to give
and those who come to take?

Dazed with your poison,
I thought he may give in,
but you let him crawl away.

Tell me – has your acidic palate
grown to dislike the taste
of the will of man?

Highbush Blueberries

I'd walked the path in my backyard
for fifteen years and never knew

the bush was there, beyond
the semi-circle stone wall –

its canes arched and gangly, crowded
by scrub oak, maple, and pine.

Sparse of leaves, never pruned
or fertilized, rooted in darkness –

it managed to bear twelve plump
blueberries, hushed and waxy,

so perfect I almost couldn't pick them.
Their cool, dusty bloom filled my palms.

I tasted one, and before I got back
to the house, they were gone –

so sweet, without a hint of bitterness.

On Coquina Beach

A tired wave crawls to shore,
draws back the shells,
deposits them, almost exactly
where they were. Unless
there's an undertow,
like the one that took my mother
years ago. Then –

everything disappears.

She never learned to swim but loves
the ocean – a small woman
who's rarely had cause
to laugh.
I warned her the undertow
could sweep her away.

And it did.

Those frozen seconds of not knowing.

I scrambled into the water,
searched the horizon,
looked left, then right –

and found her tumbling
onto the sand, twenty feet
from where she'd been – black hair
plastered to her skin,

swimsuit straps stirruped around thin arms,
coughing up the din,
and on her face – a grin!
My mother laughed.
She laughed and laughed.   I swear:

she laughed.

§

Each shell I find reminds me
of her.

Here – an augur
twisted, spiraling into the shape
of my mother's grief.

And there –
a shell I've never found before,
the lettered olive,
slender, glossy, curled
into itself,
beige with the zig-zag
pattern of a fleeing rabbit.
I wrap the shell in my fist –
make a wish

for my mother.

§

A fellow sheller asks if I've had
any luck. *In some ways,* I tell her,
holding up a lightning whelk,
covered in burnt-orange whorls, but for
the bolts that strike counterclockwise
down to a creamy point,

its aperture dark

with echo.

§

For hours I search among the ibis,
the piping plover, the sandwich tern,
the laughing gull,
until my feet become brined,

until, at last, I find my mother's
favorite delicacy – the oyster,
its shell, dull and craggy.

To her, at times, I am the irritant
that starts the pearl,
and she, at times – mine.

I cannot husk
our lifetime of nacre. Cannot trust
the recurrent dream
of us together
on Coquina Beach.

I hear my mother call, but each time,
her voice drowns
in the sound of the surf.

She, always the wave,
I, the breaking.

off balance –
redistribute
the load

Rust

At age nine, I asked my Dad
why it smelled so good
            in the autumn woods.

He inhaled so deeply, I thought
the world would disappear:

Because the leaves are dying.

I didn't fear death so much after that,
until his came seven autumns later,
          as quick as a scythe
                     to the ankles of cornstalks.

Every year since, I notice
          the asters wither,
               purple clover shrivel,
                    Boston fern burnish
     to a shade of rust.

Blight

Even though they've
stripped
my white pines of all needles –
devoured
every leaf on my pin oaks –
exposed
my once-private yard,

I save them – the squirming
caterpillars in my pool.

Doctors say it's a trauma
reaction from the time my father
beat our dog in front of me
when I was a child.
I cannot write
the details here – let's just say,
I screamed with her.

Doctors tell me the "treatment"
is to relive the trauma
over and over until
I'm no longer
sensitive – until
I no longer
panic
over suffering animals
or usher the drenched caterpillars
onto the sassafras.

Fishing

I found my little brother
and his littler friend balanced
atop a '63 Fairlane, sky-blue
and rust, windowless, sunk
halfway into the muck
of a pebbled stream.

Scrawled on the photo's bottom –
Ingonish, Summer 1978.
The boys, nearly nine with mops
of dark hair and reedy bodies,
cast fishing lines, baited
with night crawlers, toward
their slender shadows
on clear water. I wondered
what they'd caught that day –
trout, perch, sunfish, bass,
or the equally valuable – nothing.

Johnny called yesterday –
asked if I remembered when
we were kids, how we'd hid
in the crawlspace, blocked
our ears and hummed away
the violence downstairs.
"Yeah – I remember your
heartbeat against my ribs."

When words left us, I texted him
the old photo. He laughed, said,
"That's me and Kenny fishing
in Canada. When did you find that?"

I thought for a second and told him,

"In the nick of time."

Shift

I can talk

to you now, Dad,   because you /

are dead.

Sit here,   in your worn

recliner, shaped

by your great /

burden.

(Beware of his [my] body

language – the shift /

of his [my] foot,

the tremble /

of his [my] hand.)

Relax.

Before we begin, Dad, let me tell you –

I am not afraid /

of how you'll react.

If you hug me, your

ghost arms

will go right through my ribcage.

If you swing at me, your

ghost fist

will go right through my chest.

My brother named his sons after our father

or after the idea of a father.   I asked him why,

and he, eighteen months younger,

perhaps not recalling as much, perhaps

being more forgiving, wondered what I meant.

Don't you remember everything he did to us?

He answered:

Don't you?

Sea Glass

Before her husband wakes,
my friend drags out the dawn
as long as she can, walks
the beach, sifts the sand –
finds mostly shells:
spotted moon, waved whelk,
lucine, velutina.

But finding shells is too easy,
too quick – the way her husband
empties a fifth. She's looking
for glass – not the shattered kind
she sweeps off the bedroom floor,

but the kind a new tide can bring:
amber, cobalt, emerald, clear –
shards of glass once whole, cast
away – tumbled until rescued.

On days when she feels lost,
we have coffee. I watch as she
empties her pockets – drops
the sea glass into a jar on her
windowsill, promises me

she'll leave him when the jar is full.

Home

—for 238

When I return –
            I am all rib.

Mud season has ended.
I have missed
the sugaring.

My friend pulls
the maple taps
so the wounds can heal.

He offers me a free room –
says, “You’ll be safe here.”
I close the door, crumple
onto the bed – notice its
firmness, the texture
of linens, gauge the distance
between my reach
and the knife I stash
beneath the mattress.

            <>

Mist in his meadow: wild
iris blurs into daisy into trillium.
Hummingbirds sip from salvia,
bees make brief visits,

everything feeds –
and I cannot eat.

<>

In July moonlight, I wade
into my friend's pool, waist
deep – my body cleaved
by water. The unburied
half shivers,
the buried half
burns.

<>

The woods here cast shadows
in the morning. Peeling cedar,
scrub oak smothered in lichen,
feathery white pine. If I stare
long enough, they tether me
like triggers from the past –

I am trapped by the promise
of the false dawn.

<>

My ex sits on my settlement.
When I worry, my friend
holds me, tells me I can stay

forever, if I want.

I want

but cannot define my want.

I tell him this, and he feeds me
chicken francaise, glazed
carrots, herbed bread,
crème brulee.

I tell him this, and he plants me
a garden, hangs
wind chimes, buys
a rocking chair.

<>

Fridge hum
floor creak
faucet drip –
the lack of trauma
in this house unnerves me,
as do the sharp
angles of my
friend's jaw line –
the touch
of amber
in his green eyes,
the absence

of alcohol
seeping
from his pores.

I dare to hug my
less-prominent ribs.

<>

During peak foliage, we
take a drive. Route 89 curves
before us – starving for cars, cradled
by asters, chanterelles, goldenrod,
and the red, red of trees
I cannot name.

<>

In winter, when I feel idle,
he suggests, "Do what you love."
Snow gathers into smiles
on the sidelights. The howling
outside fades as snow cloaks
the house. The only sound –

his voice.

What do I love?

<>

In March, he lays his ear
on the thinning ice, hears
the Winooski River rumble.

It is time.

Together we tap the maples,
boil the sap. He offers me
a taste of syrup
from his fingertip.

It is sweet enough.

they say we do not
belong together,
but we do –
sun shower

Pointillism

—for my sister

Slowly she applies careful dots
of color to a portrait of a baby
we have yet to meet.

I ask her why she's painting
his eyes red and green –
She tells me, "You have to view

him from a distance."
I step back, squint, and see
red and green have made brown.

From here, my sister, too, looks
different. As she caresses
her rounded belly beneath

her smock, I realize she'll never
go back to being only my sister,
when she held only her paintbrush.

Nocturne

A blue-eyed daughter grows
in my womb. Within hours
she turns five. She asks me
whether the ocean eats the earth
or the earth eats the ocean.

I tell her – *We all hunger.*
I feed her apricots, oatmeal,
braid her hair, sing a lullaby:

When the dream breaks,
the cradle will fall,
and drown will come daily,
no baby – no caul.

The Childless Mother

I.

I study my only picture of you,
a black-and-white ultrasound, now faded
to a shade of bruise, pressed safely into
a dusty Bible. Your little body –
an heirloom bulb planted in fertile soil –
one that would never bloom. But for four weeks
I knew the tingle of breast, the glowing
skin, the protective hands on my still-flat
womb. As the women around me gave birth,
you became more than bulb, more than baby –
you are my evidence. I tuck you in
and close the Bible's cover – my aging
hands stained by its gilted edge, its message.

II.

The gilt is very fine and difficult
to clean. In the bathroom mirror I see
my husband's form fill the doorway. His chest
rises and falls with a swallowed sigh. He
reaches to squeeze my rigid shoulder; I
turn to the window, gaze at day lilies,
our regimented topiaries, edged
lawn, and beyond, at the neighbor's children
playing on their swing set. I hear the slow
fade of my husband's retreating footsteps
and stop drying my long-dried hands. In his

wake drifts an unspoken question: When will you learn how to let go of letting go?

Dragonflies

In the back yard, at dusk,
my eight-year-old niece
and I were caught in a whirlwind
of dragonflies – hundreds
of them swirling around us.

In that moment – in the midst
of our laughter, our long brown hair
twirling, our blue eyes – comets
in the gloaming as we danced
with the dragonflies – I imagined

she was mine.

A Childless Woman Creates Her Family Tree

By 1801, Rebekkah had delivered 14 children.
By 1910, Kathryn had seven. I discover
some ancestors with a bare branch, like mine:

Serafina, whose caller never showed,
Ruth, who took in orphans and called them her own,
Patience – barren, abandoned by her spouse –

> The preacher told her:
> pray fervently and wait.
> The healer told her:
> eat wild yams, drink waterlily tea.

When my research is done, I write my
name on the trunk because I am its
creator – the pith, the first ring.

I dwell inside the same heartwood
with Rebekkah and Kathryn,
though no baby has dwelt in me.

Nesting Season

Inspired by the line, "We are all birds looking for treetops"
— *Kevin McLellan,* "What happened in the night"

You forage and return
            to the treetop.

Despite its tapering
to an impossible thinness,
you think – *This twig will hold me.*
You

            sway,

although you feel no wind
because you have become wind.

Your feather drops –
            a swallow swoops it up,
            tucks it around her clutch –
your nest, eggless.

From the treetop, your warble carries
into the sterile dusk:

            Will my song be enough?
            Will my song be enough?

Against Desire

After the photograph, Dreamy Waterlily
— Kelly Bystrom

And why shouldn't the waterlily
guard itself against the August
swelter, the endless insect drone,
the black, stagnant water –
            against those like me

who have a small desire
to pry apart the slender fingers
of its cupped hands
to understand
            what I can never have.

I'm thankful the waterlily
is out of reach – thankful to learn
that with time, out of the muck,
the sulfurous air,
            grows grace.

anniversary visit –

his white headstone

in fresh snow

On Any Bay

Evening mist obscures
the moored boats. But we
hear their gentle rock – a faint
knock of wooden elbows,
remember the sea's debris
that flocks between them
until their next journey.

We are all
driftwood.

-ectomy

after the surgery, I grieved –

grieved for the lost

part of me,

until it became,

again, part of me.

Parts of a Letter

Twenty-seven years after his death, I receive my father's letters home from the Marine Corps (1961-63).

Envelopes:

Decomposed elastic still clings
to the stacks,
more than sixty years old –
some bordered in slashes of red,
white, and blue,
still strong
against aging cream –

others, watermarked ashen-slate with that famous photo –
U.S. Marines raising our Flag
atop Iwo Jima in World War II.

So this is what time smells like: Musk and ivory.

Dad inked his parents' address in blue.
We print the same Rs – the same Ws and Ts.

Red and white stamps on the upper right –
US Air Mail – seven cents,
postmarked:

Pray for Peace.

Stationery:

I unfold
each crease, four per page – they easily give way.
Monogrammed, 3D Marine Division, in scarlet, black, and gold,
with the Marines' emblem –
the Eagle, Anchor, Globe.

Salutation:

Dear Family,
His bass voice floats back to me –
or would it have cracked, he being fresh
out of puberty – a Marine at eighteen.

Body:

He writes perfectly parallel lines on unlined sheets.
Underneath, my fingertips feel the pressure
he placed on the pen –
his words nearly pierce
the page.

Parris Island, South Carolina

Early-September 1961:

I am with Platoon 365-Q Company. We have good equipment:
an M1 rifle, cartridge belt, bayonet, helmet, canteen.
We drill, clean barracks, study, repeat.

It's rough...the things I heard about this place are true – we had to do punishment work – 50 push-ups, talk to poles, stand at attention for an hour.

We're not allowed to laugh or smile. If we get caught, the DI makes us do push-ups while laughing.

Don't worry about me – I'm in fine health. You can't miss a day here, or you'll get behind and be sent back to another platoon.

I received very high marks on my strength tests.

Mid-September 1961:

In the hospital overnight with strep throat... will probably be sent back...have to try really hard because I missed classes...I've got to make it!

I'll make it through no matter what.

October 6-14, 1961 (from the hospital):

I have a virus – 104.8 temperature.

Boy, you civilians can't imagine how rough it is down here. Everything is double time – I haven't enough paper to tell you the rest.

October 1961:

They took our photos today. Mine came out lousy.

So handsome in his dress uniform –
white cap with black rim over high-and-tight dark hair –
flawless skin, steel-blue eyes – straight, white teeth framed
by a full-lipped smile that forms slight dimples on his face –
in the same place as mine.

October 1961:

You never say "you" to a drill instructor. If you do, they tell you they are not a female sheep, and they'll make you say "baa...baa..." while you butt your head against the wall.

If you have the least bit of rust on your rifle, you'll be sent to the brig.

When we go to physical training each day – we have to screech out everything we say and growl while we do our exercises.
Well, that's Marine life.

I've gained weight, but not an ounce of fat. I have new muscles where I've never had them before.

Ooh-rah!

The fellows here are swell guys – all of us are trying hard to be good Marines.

A kid cut off his fingers with a bayonet because he wanted to get out of the Marine Corps.

My platoon is dwindling.

October 1961:

Drownproofing...It is exactly what it sounds like.
I passed my swimming test – only 16 out of 81 made it. The Marines certainly are a good outfit. It's hard and all, but you become proud that you're a part of it.

October 23, 1961:

We're staying in Quonset huts because we're going to the rifle range tomorrow.

Some guy tried to escape the island and drowned.

The Drill Instructor told us about Vietnam.

October 27, 1961:

I qualified– shot the M1, a .45 pistol, and a Browning Automatic. Will be getting an expert marksmanship medal.

November 24, 1961:

I graduate tomorrow with my original platoon.

Camp LeJeune, North Carolina:

November 30, 1961:

This is the place where you learn how to kill a man.

December 1961:

I was chosen to be a Fire Team Leader. That doesn't mean I put out fires. I direct my men into position to fight the enemy.

We did the infiltration course with live machine gun fire – if we'd stood up we'd have gotten killed – went through booby traps and into a gas chamber with no mask. Everyone got sick.

Camp Geiger, North Carolina:

January 1962:

I can hardly pick up this damn pen. Everyone in my company is so tired, that it isn't funny.

I am singing with a group of boys; we sound real good.

Camp Pendleton, California:

March 8, 1962:

I have me a stripe now – I'm really happy!

March 10, 1962:

The news has just been passed to pack sea bags and be ready to go by tomorrow.

Camp Schwab, Okinawa, Japan:

April 1962:

Hit a bad storm – waves going over the ship. We crossed the International Time Zone and were initiated into King Neptune's Cult.

We work 18 hours a day. I'm getting real tired.

May 1962:

Got your letter. I wish you wouldn't worry.

June 1962:

I came in first in all three events of the strength tests.

I'm on the baseball team – I play left field and center field, and bat clean-up.

I bought a $41 Bible and still go to church on Sundays.

July 23, 1962:

I earned my High School Diploma. I might go to either Boston

University or Northeastern when I get home. Might want to be a private investigator or a professional bassist.

August 1962:

We are doing guerrilla war training in the jungle – got thousands of mosquito bites – it's 110 degrees out.

Camp Hansen, Okinawa, Japan:

October 26, 1962:

As you probably know, there's some trouble with Cuba and Russia. We were given the alert.

Buy Christmas gifts for the family with the money I'm sending home.

<u>Valediction</u>:

December 1962:

Letter from the U.S. Naval Hospital, Philadelphia, PA, to my father's parents:

Your son has been admitted for a period of observation and hospitalization for certain emotional problems that he was presenting at his duty station.

Medical Records, U.S. Naval Hospital, Philadelphia, PA:

Nineteen-year-old, single, Caucasian male...was admitted to the sick list at the U. S. Army Hospital, San Francisco, California, with the diagnosis of Schizophrenic Reaction. The patient while on liberty became assaultive while drinking in a bar.

"I didn't mean it...My mind is all mixed up...someone's got to help me, sir."

December 1962:

Letter home:

I'll try to call you up on Christmas...I'm feeling better.

December 26, 1962:

Don't worry about me, as I shall get better minute by minute, day by day.

February 15, 1963:

Report of Board of Medical Survey:

The patient is in a state of relative remission. The Board recommends that he be discharged from the U. S. Marine Corps. There is no disciplinary action pending.

Postscript:

Oh, Marine
Shellback
Expert Marksman
Fire Team Leader

Traveler
Athlete
Singer
Socializer

Father,

I speak to you, now – the man who couldn't leave our house,
yet traveled farther than I've ever been.

At this moment, I don't care about the wrongs you committed.

I wish I could cook for you – something rich and time-consuming –
lasagna, turkey dinner, lobster bisque, bouillabaisse, Italian cream cake.
I would serve you
at the head of the table, where you'd take a bite
and your steel-blue eyes would meet mine, and you'd smile –
tell me everything was delicious.

But I must settle for this:
I place your last letter atop the stack on my lap –
pull them to my chest – compress
their crisp loft – inhale

their exhalation.

ACKNOWLEDGMENTS

The author gratefully acknowledges the editors of the following journals, who first published these poems, some in previous versions or under different titles:

The American Journal of Poetry and MassPoetry.org ("Poem of the Moment"): "My father drew maps"
Avalon Literary Review: "Northern Lights"
Burningword Literary Journal: "Mum says don't swallow gum or it will stay in your stomach for seven years"
The Chaffin Journal: Excerpt from "Parts of a Letter," "Rust," and "Blight"
Common Ground Review: "350s," "Nocturne"
The Comstock Review: "The Childless Mother"
Evening Street Review: "My brother named his sons after our father"
50 Haikus: "anniversary visit"
45th Parallel: "On Coquina Beach"
The Poetry Project – Ireland: "To the Bog of Allen"
Puckerbrush Review: "so many bleeding hearts"
Summer, Still: "350s"
Tiger's Eye: A Journal of Poetry: "Sea Glass"

SPECIAL THANKS

To my family – still together, despite the chaos, and to my husband for his unfailing support. My sincere appreciation to the talented editorial team at Lily Poetry Review Books, in particular, Eileen Cleary, for her encouragement, insights, and ceaseless work, and Michael McInnis for his cover art design. I am grateful to the Solstice MFA Program community: The directors, the brilliant faculty (including my mentors, Dzvinia Orlowsky, Iain Haley Pollock, Laure-Anne Bosselaar, Kathleen Aguero, and Nicole Terez Dutton), and my workshop peers, plus the Gardner porch gang, without whom this book would not be possible. Thanks also to my incredible writer friends – Louise Viera, the late Professor Emeritus John Pollock, Jenifer DeBellis, Professor John Mulrooney, Roselyn Kubek, Leanna Hamill, Brian Mosher, Mark Walsh, Alison Cappella, Emily Jane VandenBos Style, Miriam O'Neal, PTAOW, and the members of the former Tidepool Poets, for their careful readings and thoughtful suggestions, or for just listening. Lastly, my affection and thanks to my long-time friends, from as far back as grade school, for your comfort and laughter – there are too many of you to list (lucky me!).

ABOUT THE AUTHOR

Lisa J. Sullivan is a New England native who holds an MFA in Poetry from the Solstice MFA in Creative Writing Program, where she was a Kurt Brown Memorial Fellow. Her poems, book reviews, and artist interviews have been widely published. She was the United States winner of The Poetry Project–Ireland in collaboration with the Academy of American Poets and was an Adrian Tinsley Program Creative Grant recipient. Lisa is the Art Editor for *Lily Poetry Review* and a Poetry Editor for *Pink Panther Magazine*. *Theory of Impact* is her debut poetry collection.

www.ingramcontent.com/pod-product-compliance
Lightning Source LLC
Chambersburg PA
CBHW021344060726
47591CB00006B/2161

* 9 7 8 1 9 5 7 7 5 5 7 7 9 *